LIFE
Lessons

REVELATION

MAX
LUCADO

REVELATION

MAX
LUCADO

LIFE
Lessons

WITH MAX LUCADO

BOOK OF
REVELATION

FINAL CURTAIN CALL

MAX LUCADO

Prepared by

THE LIVINGSTONE CORPORATION

THOMAS NELSON
Since 1798

NASHVILLE   DALLAS   MEXICO CITY   RIO DE JANEIRO

Life Lessons with Max Lucado—Book of Revelation

© 2006, Nelson Impact

Published in Nashville, Tennessee, by Thomas Nelson. Thomas Nelson is a registered trademark of Thomas Nelson, Inc.

Produced with the assistance of the Livingstone Corporation (www.livingstonecorp.com). Project staff include Jake Barton, Joel Bartlett, Andy Culbertson, Mary Horner Collins, and Will Reaves.

Editor: Neil Wilson

Scripture quotations marked "NCV™" are taken from the New Century Version®. © 2005 by Thomas Nelson, Inc. Used by permission. All rights reserved.

Scripture quotations marked "NKJV™" are taken from the New King James Version®. © 1982 by Thomas Nelson, Inc. Used by permission. All rights reserved.

Scripture quotations marked (MSG) are taken from *THE MESSAGE*. © 1993, 1994, 1995, 1996, 2000, 2001, 2002 by Eugene H. Peterson. Used by permission of NavPress Publishing Group.

Scripture quotations marked (NIV) are taken from the Holy Bible, New International Version. © 1973, 1978, 1984 by International Bible Society. All rights reserved. Used by permission of Zondervan Publishing House.

Material for the "Inspiration" sections taken from the following books:

And the Angels Were Silent. © 2004 by Max Lucado. W Publishing Group, a Division of Thomas Nelson, Inc., Nashville, Tennessee.

The Applause of Heaven. © 1990, 1996, 1999 by Max Lucado. W Publishing Group, a Division of Thomas Nelson, Inc., Nashville, Tennessee.

The Great House of God. © 1997 by Max Lucado. W Publishing Group, a Division of Thomas Nelson, Inc., Nashville, Tennessee.

In the Eye of the Storm. © 1991 by Max Lucado. W Publishing Group, a Division of Thomas Nelson, Inc., Nashville, Tennessee.

It's Not About Me. © 2004 by Max Lucado. Integrity Publishers, Brentwood, Tennessee.

Shaped by God (previously published as *On the Anvil*). © 2001 by Max Lucado. Tyndale House Publishers, Wheaton, Illinois.

Traveling Light. © 2001 by Max Lucado. W Publishing Group, a Division of Thomas Nelson, Inc., Nashville, Tennessee.

When Christ Comes. © 1999 by Max Lucado. W Publishing Group, a Division of Thomas Nelson, Inc., Nashville, Tennessee.

Cover Art and Interior Design by Kirk Luttrell of the Livingstone Corporation

Interior Composition by Rachel Hawkins of the Livingstone Corporation

ISBN: 978-1-4185-0958-3

Printed in the United States of America.

HB 04.30.2018

WITH MAX LUCADO

CONTENTS

HOW TO
STUDY THE BIBLE

This is a peculiar book you are holding. Words crafted in another language. Deeds done in a distant era. Events recorded in a far-off land. Counsel offered to a foreign people. This is a peculiar book.

It's surprising that anyone reads it. It's too old. Some of its writings date back five thousand years. It's too bizarre. The book speaks of incredible floods, fires, earthquakes, and people with supernatural abilities. It's too radical. The Bible calls for undying devotion to a carpenter who called himself God's Son.

Logic says this book shouldn't survive. Too old, too bizarre, too radical.

The Bible has been banned, burned, scoffed, and ridiculed. Scholars have mocked it as foolish. Kings have branded it as illegal. A thousand times over, the grave has been dug and the dirge has begun, but somehow the Bible never stays in the grave. Not only has it survived; it has thrived. It is the single most popular book in all of history. It has been the best-selling book in the world for years!

There is no way on earth to explain it. Which perhaps is the only explanation. The answer? The Bible's durability is not found on earth; it is found in heaven. For the millions who have tested its claims and claimed its promises, there is but one answer: the Bible is God's book and God's voice.

As you read it, you would be wise to give some thought to two questions. What is the purpose of the Bible? and How do I study the Bible? Time spent reflecting on these two issues will greatly enhance your Bible study.

What is the purpose of the Bible?

Let the Bible itself answer that question.

Since you were a child you have known the Holy Scriptures which are able to make you wise. And that wisdom leads to salvation through faith in Christ Jesus. (2 Tim. 3:15 NCV)

The purpose of the Bible? Salvation. God's highest passion is to get his children home. His book, the Bible, describes his plan of salvation. The purpose of the Bible is to proclaim God's plan and passion to save his children.

That is the reason this book has endured through the centuries. It dares to tackle the toughest questions about life: Where do I go after I die? Is there a God? What do I do with my fears? The Bible offers answers to these crucial questions. It is the treasure map that leads us to God's highest treasure, eternal life.

But how do we use the Bible? Countless copies of Scripture sit unread on bookshelves and nightstands simply because people don't know how to read it. What can we do to make the Bible real in our lives?

The clearest answer is found in the words of Jesus. He promised:

Ask, and God will give to you. Search, and you will find. Knock, and the door will open for you. (Matt. 7:7 NCV)

The first step in understanding the Bible is asking God to help us. We should read prayerfully. If anyone understands God's Word, it is because of God and not the reader.

But the Helper will teach you everything and will cause you to remember all that I told you. The Helper is the Holy Spirit whom the Father will send in my name. (John 14:26 NCV)

Before reading the Bible, pray. Invite God to speak to you. Don't go to Scripture looking for your idea; go searching for his.

Not only should we read the Bible prayerfully; we should read it carefully. *Search and you will find* is the pledge. The Bible is not a newspaper to be skimmed but rather a mine to be quarried.

Search for it like silver, and hunt for it like hidden treasure. Then you will understand respect for the LORD, and you will find that you know God. (Prov. 2:4–5 NCV)

Any worthy find requires effort. The Bible is no exception. To understand the Bible you don't have to be brilliant, but you must be willing to roll up your sleeves and search.

Be a worker who is not ashamed and who uses the true teaching in the right way. (2 Tim. 2:15 NCV)

Here's a practical point. Study the Bible a bit at a time. Hunger is not satisfied by eating twenty-one meals in one sitting once a week. The body needs a steady diet to remain strong. So does the soul. When God sent food to his people in the wilderness, he didn't provide loaves already made. Instead, he sent them manna in the shape of *"thin flakes like frost . . . on the desert ground"* (Ex. 16:14 NCV).

God gave manna in limited portions. God sends spiritual food the same way. He opens the heavens with just enough nutrients for today's hunger. He provides *"a command here, a command there. A rule here, a rule there. A little lesson here, a little lesson there"* (Isa. 28:10 NCV).

Don't be discouraged if your reading reaps a small harvest. Some days a lesser portion is all that is needed. What is important is to search every day for that day's message. A steady diet of God's Word over a lifetime builds a healthy soul and mind.

A little girl returned from her first day at school. Her mom asked, "Did you learn anything?"

"Apparently not enough," the girl responded, "I have to go back tomorrow and the next day and the next . . ."

Such is the case with learning. And such is the case with Bible study. Understanding comes little by little over a lifetime.

There is a third step in understanding the Bible. After the asking and seeking comes the knocking. After you ask and search, then knock.

Knock, and the door will open for you. (Matt. 7:7 NCV)

To knock is to stand at God's door. To make yourself available. To climb the steps, cross the porch, stand at the doorway, and volunteer. Knocking goes beyond the realm of thinking and into the realm of acting.

To knock is to ask, What can I do? How can I obey? Where can I go?

It's one thing to know what to do. It's another to do it. But for those who do it, those who choose to obey, a special reward awaits them.

The truly happy are those who carefully study God's perfect law that makes people free, and they continue to study it. They do not forget what they heard, but they obey what God's teaching says. Those who do this will be made happy. (James 1:25 NCV)

What a promise. Happiness comes to those who do what they read! It's the same with medicine. If you only read the label but ignore the pills, it won't help. It's the same with food. If you only read the recipe but never cook, you won't be fed. And it's the same with the Bible. If you only read the words but never obey, you'll never know the joy God has promised.

Ask. Search. Knock. Simple, isn't it? Why don't you give it a try? If you do, you'll see why you are holding the most remarkable book in history.

INTRODUCTION TO THE BOOK OF REVELATION

An ancient legend tells of a general whose army was afraid to fight. The soldiers were frightened. The enemy was too strong. Their fortress was too high and weapons too mighty.

The king, however, was not afraid. He knew his men would win. How could he convince them?

He had an idea. He told his soldiers that he possessed a magical coin. A prophetic coin. A coin which would foretell the outcome of the battle. On one side was an eagle and on the other a bear. He would toss the coin. If it landed eagle-side up, they would win. If it landed with the bear up, they would lose.

The army was silent as the coin flipped in the air. Soldiers circled as it fell to the ground. They held their breath as they looked and shouted when they saw the eagle. The army would win.

Bolstered by the assurance of victory, the men marched against the castle and won.

It was only after the victory that the king showed the men the coin. The two sides were identical.

Though the story is fictional, the truth is reliable: assured victory empowers the army.

That may be the reason God gives us the book of Revelation. In it he assures victory. We, the soldiers, are privileged a glimpse into the final battlefield. All hell breaks loose as all heaven comes forth. The two collide in the ultimate battle of good and evil. Left standing amid the smoke and thunder is the Son of God. Jesus, born in a manger, is now triumphant over Satan.

Satan is defeated. Christ is triumphant. And we, the soldiers, are assured of victory.

Let us march.

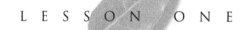

LESSON ONE

A VISION
OF CHRIST

MAX
LUCADO

REFLECTION

Reunions with old friends or family create a variety of feelings. They bring old memories up to the moment. They also correct our imaginations. Think of a time when you saw a friend you hadn't seen in a long time. How had that person changed? What did you discover from that encounter?

SITUATION

The apostle John was the author of the Gospel of John and the three epistles of John. He served in the church in Ephesus before he was arrested by the Roman authorities. The last living representative of Jesus' twelve disciples, he was exiled and alone on the island of Patmos. We don't know how he was feeling, but we do know that he was spending time in worship when he experienced an amazing vision.

OBSERVATION

Read Revelation 1:9–20 from the NCV or the NKJV.

NCV

9I, John, am your brother. All of us share with Christ in suffering, in the kingdom, and in patience to continue. I was on the island of Patmos, because I had preached the word of God and the message about Jesus. 10On the Lord's day I was in the Spirit, and I heard a loud voice behind me that sounded like a trumpet. 11The voice said, "Write what you see in a book and send it to the seven churches: to Ephesus, Smyrna, Pergamum, Thyatira, Sardis, Philadelphia, and Laodicea."

12I turned to see who was talking to me. When I turned, I saw seven golden lampstands 13and someone among the lampstands who was "like a Son of Man." He was dressed in a long robe and had a gold band around his chest. 14His head and hair were white like wool, as white as snow, and his eyes were like flames of fire. 15His feet were like bronze that glows hot in a furnace, and his voice was like the noise of flooding water. 16He held seven stars in his right hand, and a sharp double-edged sword came out of his mouth. He looked like the sun shining at its brightest time.

17When I saw him, I fell down at his feet like a dead man. He put his right hand on me and said, "Do not be afraid. I am the First and the Last. 18I am the One who lives; I was dead, but look, I am alive forever and ever! And I hold the keys to death and to the place of the dead. 19So write the things you see, what is now and what will happen later. 20Here is the secret of the seven stars that you saw in my right hand and the seven golden lampstands: The seven lampstands are the seven churches, and the seven stars are the angels of the seven churches.

NKJV

9I, John, both your brother and companion in the tribulation and kingdom and patience of Jesus Christ, was on the island that is called Patmos for the word of God and for the testimony of Jesus Christ. 10I was in the Spirit on the Lord's Day, and I heard behind me a loud voice, as of a trumpet, 11saying, "I am the Alpha and the Omega, the First and the Last," and, "What you see, write in a book and send it to the seven churches which are in Asia: to Ephesus, to Smyrna, to Pergamos, to Thyatira, to Sardis, to Philadelphia, and to Laodicea."

12Then I turned to see the voice that spoke with me. And having turned I saw seven golden lampstands, 13and in the midst of the seven lampstands One like the Son of Man, clothed with a garment down to the feet and girded about the chest with a golden band. 14His head and hair were white like wool, as white as snow, and His eyes like a flame of fire; 15His feet were like fine brass, as if refined in a furnace, and His voice as the sound of many waters; 16He had in His right hand seven stars, out of His mouth went a sharp two-edged sword, and His countenance was like the sun shining in its strength.

[17]And when I saw Him, I fell at His feet as dead. But He laid His right hand on me, saying to me, "Do not be afraid; I am the First and the Last. [18]I am He who lives, and was dead, and behold, I am alive forevermore. Amen. And I have the keys of Hades and of Death. [19]Write the things which you have seen, and the things which are, and the things which will take place after this. [20]The mystery of the seven stars which you saw in My right hand, and the seven golden lampstands: The seven stars are the angels of the seven churches, and the seven lampstands which you saw are the seven churches."

EXPLORATION

1. Why do you think the churches are symbolized as lampstands?

2. In what ways do you think John's vision of Jesus differs from the Jesus he knew in person?

3. How do you think John felt to see Christ again?

4. Why was John told to write down the things he saw?

5. How would you respond if you saw someone whose feet were like bronze and eyes were like fire?

INSPIRATION

You are in your car driving home. Thoughts wander to the game you want to see or meal you want to eat, when suddenly a sound unlike any you've ever heard fills the air. The sound is high above you. A trumpet? A choir? A choir of trumpets? You don't know, but you want to know. So you pull over, get out of your car, and look up. As you do, you see you aren't the only curious one. The roadside has become a parking lot. Car doors are open, and people are staring at the sky. Shoppers are racing out of the grocery store. The Little League baseball game across the street has come to a halt. Players and parents are searching the clouds.

And what they see, and what you see, has never before been seen.

As if the sky were a curtain, the drapes of the atmosphere part. A brilliant light spills onto the earth. There are no shadows. None. From whence came the light begins to tumble a river of color—spiking crystals of every hue ever seen and a million more never seen. Riding on the flow is an endless fleet of angels. They pass through the curtain one myriad at a time, until they occupy every square inch of the sky. North. South. East. West. Thousands of silvery wings rise and fall in unison, and over the sound of the trumpets, you can hear the cherubim and seraphim chanting, "Holy, holy, holy."

The final flank of angels is followed by twenty-four silver-bearded elders and a multitude of souls who join the angels in worship. Presently the movement stops and the trumpets are silent, leaving only the triumphant triplet: "Holy, holy, holy." Between each word is a pause. With each word, a profound reverence. You hear your voice join in the chorus. You don't know why you say the words, but you know you must.

Suddenly the heavens are quiet. All is quiet. The angels turn, you turn, the entire world turns—and there he is. Jesus. Through waves of light you see the silhouetted figure of Christ the King. He is atop a great stallion, and the stallion is atop a billowing cloud. He opens his mouth, and you are surrounded by his declaration: "I am the Alpha and the Omega."

The angels bow their heads. The elders remove their crowns. And before you is a figure so consuming that you know, instantly you know: Nothing else matters. Forget stock markets and school reports. Sales meetings and football games. Nothing is newsworthy. All that mattered, matters no more, for Christ has come. (From *When Christ Comes* by Max Lucado)

REACTION

6. In what way is John's vision in Revelation different from the image of Jesus in your mind?

7. In what way does John's vision change your image of Christ?

8. What does this vision do for your relationship with Christ?

9. Why do we no longer need to fear death after reading a passage like this?

10. How can this vision be an encouragement if you are facing difficult times?

11. How can you help someone have a new awareness of Christ and his power?

LIFE LESSONS

God is never limited by our circumstances and often uses them for his purposes. When we're isolated, we're less distracted. Just as he did with John, God sometimes puts us in places where we will pay attention to his voice. We need to take our mental and painted pictures of Jesus lightly, but hold dearly to the composite impression of his majesty, character, authority, and beauty. Like John, we don't worship idols or images, but Christ in the Spirit.

DEVOTION

Lord Jesus, you are more powerful than we could ever imagine. We stand in awe of your presence and fall at your feet in worship. To you be glory and authority forever and ever.

For more Bible passages on Christ's authority and power, see Luke 4:36; 1 Corinthians 15:22–24; 2 Corinthians 10:4–5; Ephesians 1:19–21; Colossians 2:9–12.

To complete the book of Revelation during this twelve-part study, read Revelation 1:1–20.

JOURNALING

In light of this vision, how will I live differently?

LESSON TWO

YOUR FIRST LOVE

MAX
LUCADO

REFLECTION

Think back to the first time you fell head over heels in love. List some of the odd things that falling in love made you do. Think about the (at least temporary) improvements it brought about in you. What do you remember most about your first love?

SITUATION

After appearing to John in a vision, Jesus instructed him to write a memo to each of seven churches in an area we now know as Turkey. The sequence of these letters follows a rough geographic circle formed by the cities mentioned. These were spiritual-health evaluations. For experienced readers of the New Testament, only the first church is well-known: Ephesus.

OBSERVATION

Read Revelation 2:1–7 from the NCV or the NKJV.

NCV

[1]"Write this to the angel of the church in Ephesus:

"The One who holds the seven stars in his right hand and walks among the seven golden lampstands says this: [2]I know what you do, how you work hard and never give up. I know you do not put up with the false teachings of evil people. You have tested those who say they are apostles but really are not, and you found they are liars. [3]You have patience and have suffered troubles for my name and have not given up.

[4]"But I have this against you: You have left the love you had in the beginning. [5]So remember where you were before you fell. Change your hearts and do what you did at first. If you do not change, I will come to you and will take away your lampstand from its place. [6]But there is something you do that is right: You hate what the Nicolaitans do, as much as I.

[7]"Every person who has ears should listen to what the Spirit says to the churches. To those who win the victory I will give the right to eat the fruit from the tree of life, which is in the garden of God.

NKJV

[1]"To the angel of the church of Ephesus write,

'These things says He who holds the seven stars in His right hand, who walks in the midst of the seven golden lampstands: [2]"I know your works, your labor, your patience, and that you cannot bear those who are evil. And you have tested those who say they are apostles and are not, and have found them liars; [3]and you have persevered and have patience, and have labored for My name's sake and have not become weary. [4]Nevertheless I have this against you, that you have left your first love. [5]Remember therefore from where you have fallen; repent and do the first works, or else I will come to you quickly and remove your lampstand from its place—unless you repent. [6]But this you have, that you hate the deeds of the Nicolaitans, which I also hate.

[7]"He who has an ear, let him hear what the Spirit says to the churches. To him who overcomes I will give to eat from the tree of life, which is in the midst of the Paradise of God.'"

EXPLORATION

1. Christ was pleased that the church of Ephesus didn't give up. Why did this please him?

2. What was lacking from the labor and patience of the Ephesian church?

3. In what ways could the Ephesians reconcile themselves to God?

4. What do you think it means that their lampstand would be removed from its place?

5. Why would their lampstand be removed if they didn't repent?

INSPIRATION

What Copernicus did for the earth, God does for our souls. Tapping the collective shoulder of humanity, he points to the Son—his Son—and says, "Behold the center of it all."

"God raised him [Christ] from death and set him on a throne in deep heaven, in charge of running the universe, everything from galaxies to governments, no name and no power exempt from his rule. And not just for the time being but forever. He is in charge of it all, has the final word on everything. At the center of all this, Christ rules the church" (Eph. 1:20-22 MSG).

When God looks at the center of the universe, he doesn't look at you. When heaven's stagehands direct the spotlight toward the star of the show, I need no sunglasses. No light falls on me.

Lesser orbs, that's us. Appreciated. Valued. Loved dearly. But central? Essential? Pivotal? Nope. Sorry. Contrary to the Ptolemy within us, the world does not revolve around us. Our comfort is not God's priority. If it is, something's gone awry. If we are the marquee event, how do we explain flat-earth challenges like death, disease, slumping economies, or rumbling earthquakes? If God exists to please us, then shouldn't we always be pleased?

Could a Copernican shift be in order? Perhaps our place is not at the center of the universe. God does not exist to make a big deal out of us. We exist to make a big deal out of him. It's not about you. It's not about me. It's all about him.

The moon models our role.

What does the moon do? She generates no light. Contrary to the lyrics of the song, this harvest moon cannot shine on. Apart from the sun, the moon is nothing more than a pitch-black, pockmarked rock. But properly positioned, the moon beams. Let her do what she was made to do, and a clod of dirt becomes a source of inspiration, yea, verily, romance. The moon reflects a greater light.

And she's happy to do so! You never hear the moon complaining. She makes no waves about making waves. Let the cow jump over her or astronauts step on her; she never objects. Even though sunning is accepted while mooning is the butt of bad jokes, you won't hear ol' Cheese-face grumble. The moon is at peace in her place. And because she is, soft light touches a dark earth.

What would happen if we accepted our place as Son reflectors? (From *It's Not About Me* by Max Lucado)

REACTION

6. Do you find it tempting to play the part of the sun in your universe, rather than the moon? In what ways has your love for God changed since you became a Christian?

7. How can you reignite the flames of your love for Christ? What direction can you find in this lesson's passage?

8. Is it possible to keep your love for God intense and enthusiastic?

9. What are some practical ways to keep your relationship with God a top priority?

10. In what ways can you motivate others to renew their relationship with Christ?

11. What does God's reaction to this church show about his feelings for the universal church in general?

LIFE LESSONS

Most of us tend to drift from our "first love." We may still be busy doing the "works" that Jesus noted, but our hearts aren't in the relationship. We're distracted. We've drifted. Acknowledging the loss is the first important step back toward love. The next step is to identify how our "works" have changed. Jesus complimented the present works of the Ephesians; but he pointed out that they had stopped their "first works." What did our original encounter with Jesus inspire us to do, and how much of it have we stopped doing?

DEVOTION

Jesus, forgive us for straying from our first love. Help us renew our commitment to you, and bring us back into a right relationship with you. Bring honor and glory to yourself through our lives.

For more Bible passages on putting God first, see Deuteronomy 5:7; Judges 17:6; 1 Samuel 14:36; Psalm 86:11; Matthew 6:33.

To complete the book of Revelation during this twelve-part study, read Revelation 2:1–11.

JOURNALING

What is motivating my service and sacrifice for God?

LESSON THREE

NO
COMPROMISE

MAX
LUCADO

REFLECTION

The desire for acceptance can take on magneticlike power. We may find ourselves attracted to behavior, dress, or language simply because we want to be accepted by the group around us. Compromise starts to happen. Think of a time when you did something just to fit in. What was the result?

SITUATION

As John's vision continued, Jesus spoke words to the church in Smyrna that suffered persecution and material poverty. He was aware of their difficulties but informed them that those hardships were not over. He called them to faithfulness. Then Jesus turned to the church at Pergamum, the object of this lesson. This church included several groups whose teachings ran contrary to what Christ taught. You may have to do some background work to identify the teaching of Balaam and the Nicolaitans.

OBSERVATION

Read Revelation 2:12–17 from the NCV or the NKJV.

NCV

12"Write this to the angel of the church in Pergamum:

"The One who has the sharp, double-edged sword says this: *13*I know where you live. It is where Satan has his throne. But you are true to me. You did not refuse to tell about your faith in me even during the time of Antipas, my faithful witness who was killed in your city, where Satan lives.

14"But I have a few things against you: You have some there who follow the teaching of Balaam. He taught Balak how to cause the people of Israel to sin by eating food offered to idols and by taking part in sexual sins. *15*You also have some who follow the teaching of the Nicolaitans. *16*So change your hearts and lives. If you do not, I will come to you quickly and fight against them with the sword that comes out of my mouth.

17"Everyone who has ears should listen to what the Spirit says to the churches.

"I will give some of the hidden manna to everyone who wins the victory. I will also give to each one who wins the victory a white stone with a new name written on it. No one knows this new name except the one who receives it.

NKJV

12"And to the angel of the church in Pergamos write,

'These things says He who has the sharp two-edged sword: *13*I know your works, and where you dwell, where Satan's throne is. And you hold fast to My name, and did not deny My faith even in the days in which Antipas was My faithful martyr, who was killed among you, where Satan dwells. *14*But I have a few things against you, because you have there those who hold the doctrine of Balaam, who taught Balak to put a stumbling block before the children of Israel, to eat things sacrificed to idols, and to commit sexual immorality. *15*Thus you also have those who hold the doctrine of the Nicolaitans, which thing I hate. *16*Repent, or else I will come to you quickly and will fight against them with the sword of My mouth.

*17*He who has an ear, let him hear what the Spirit says to the churches. To him who overcomes I will give some of the hidden manna to eat. And I will give him a white stone, and on the stone a new name written which no one knows except him who receives it.'"

EXPLORATION

1. How had the church in Pergamos demonstrated their faith in Christ?

2. What fault did Christ find with the church in Pergamos?

3. What temptations might the church members have had to face living in Pergamos, a city of idol worship?

4. Some people in the church in Pergamos ate food offered to idols. How was this a destructive compromise?

5. How do you strike the balance between being enough a part of your community to evangelize and keeping yourself separate from sin?

INSPIRATION

The empty tomb did not erase the crowing rooster. Christ had returned, but Peter wondered, he must have wondered, "After what I did, would he return for someone like me?"

We've wondered the same. Is Peter the only person to do the very thing he swore he'd never do?

"Infidelity is behind me!"

"From now on, I'm going to bridle my tongue."

"No more shady deals. I've learned my lesson."

Oh, the volume of our boasting. And, oh, the heartbreak of our shame.

Rather than resist the flirting, we return to it.

Rather than ignore the gossip, we share it.

Rather than stick to the truth, we shade it.

And the rooster crows, and conviction pierces, and Peter has a partner in the shadows. We weep as Peter wept, and we do what Peter did. We go fishing. We go back to our old lives. We return to our pre-Jesus practices. We do what comes naturally, rather than what comes spiritually. And we question whether Jesus has a place for folks like us.

Jesus answers that question. He answers it for you and me and all who tend to "Peter out" on Christ. His answer came on the shore of the sea in a gift to Peter. You know what Jesus did? Split the waters? Turn the boat to gold and the nets to silver? No, Jesus did something much more meaningful. He invited Peter to breakfast. Jesus prepared a meal.

Of course the breakfast was one special moment among several that morning. There was the great catch of fish and the recognition of Jesus. The plunge of Peter and the paddling of the disciples. And there was the moment they reached the shore and found Jesus next to a fire of coals. The fish were sizzling, and the bread was waiting, and the defeater of hell and the ruler of heaven invited his friends to sit down and have a bit to eat.

No one could have been more grateful than Peter. The one Satan had sifted like wheat was eating bread at the hand of God. Peter was welcomed to the meal of Christ. Right there for the devil and his tempters to see, Jesus "prepared a table in the presence of his enemies."

OK, so maybe Peter didn't say it that way. But David did. *"You prepare a table before me in the presence of my enemies"* (Ps. 23:5 NKJV). What the shepherd did for the sheep sounds a lot like what Jesus did for Peter. (From *Traveling Light* by Max Lucado)

REACTION

6. What temptations do you deal with on a regular basis that might cause you to compromise your faith?

7. In what ways can you have a relationship with someone of a different faith without compromising your own beliefs?

8. How do you deal with the shortcomings and compromises that are part of your experience?

9. List some ways you can prevent yourself from compromising your faith and morals. How do past failures affect your effectiveness? (See the excerpt above.)

10. In what ways have churches in history compromised for the world's acceptance?

11. What stumbling blocks could Satan place in your church?

LIFE LESSONS

Some compromises surprise us; others lay siege to our souls. Sometimes we fold; sometimes we hold—for a while. Some of us, like those mentioned in the quote from *Traveling Light*, live under a cloud of remorse over past compromises or fear about the future. But let that regret or fear serve as impetus for us to return to the Lord. What we need to remember is that as soon as we turn around and run to him, God meets us with open arms.

DEVOTION

Dear Father, we are so easily swayed by this world and its thinking. Forgive us when we compromise our faith. Help us stand firm as we face the many stumbling blocks ahead of us.

For more Bible passages on compromise, see Exodus 8:25–29; Numbers 25:1–2; 1 Kings 11:3–4; Ezra 4:1–3; 9:1–2; Daniel 1:1–23; 2 Corinthians 6:14–18.

To complete the book of Revelation during this twelve-part study, read Revelation 2:12–17.

JOURNALING

Are there any ways that I subtly compromise my beliefs in order to be accepted?

L E S S O N   F O U R

STANDING
AGAINST
CORRUPTION

MAX
LUCADO

REFLECTION

Our ability to discern between safety and danger, food and poison, right and wrong, true and false is necessary for physical and spiritual health. We have to learn *how* to discern as well as *when* to discern. Think of a time when you needed to discern if something was authentic or counterfeit, or if something was true or false. How did you determine the difference?

- Gut
- Facts
- Plausability

SITUATION

Thyatira was the fourth church on the Lord's list. Again, the review was mixed. Jesus noted an increase in their good works, but he confronted a significant underlying problem. They had been taken in by a charismatic figure spreading false teaching. Jesus appealed to his followers in this church to "hold fast" to what was right.

OBSERVATION

Read Revelation 2:18–29 from the NCV or the NKJV.

NCV

18"Write this to the angel of the church in Thyatira:

"The Son of God, who has eyes that blaze like fire and feet like shining bronze, says this: 19I know what you do. I know about your love, your faith, your service, and your patience. I know that you are doing more now than you did at first.

20"But I have this against you: You let that woman Jezebel spread false teachings. She says she is a prophetess, but by her teaching she leads my people to take part in sexual sins and to eat food that is offered to idols. ²¹I have given her time to change her heart and turn away from her sin, but she does not want to change. ²²So I will throw her on a bed of suffering. And all those who take part in adultery with her will suffer greatly if they do not turn away from the wrongs she does. ²³I will also kill her followers. Then all the churches will know I am the One who searches hearts and minds, and I will repay each of you for what you have done.

²⁴"But others of you in Thyatira have not followed her teaching and have not learned what some call Satan's deep secrets. I say to you that I will not put any other load on you. ²⁵Only continue in your loyalty until I come.

²⁶"I will give power over the nations to everyone who wins the victory and continues to be obedient to me until the end.

²⁷'You will rule over them with an iron rod,

as when pottery is broken into pieces.'

²⁸This is the same power I received from my Father. I will also give him the morning star. ²⁹Everyone who has ears should listen to what the Spirit says to the churches."

NKJV

¹⁸"And to the angel of the church in Thyatira write,

'These things says the Son of God, who has eyes like a flame of fire, and His feet like fine brass: ¹⁹I know your works, love, service, faith, and your patience; and as for your works, the last are more than the first. ²⁰Nevertheless I have a few things against you, because you allow that woman Jezebel, who calls herself a prophetess, to teach and seduce My servants to commit sexual immorality and eat things sacrificed to idols. ²¹And I gave her time to repent of her sexual immorality, and she did not repent. ²²Indeed I will cast her into a sickbed, and those who commit adultery with her into great tribulation, unless they repent of their deeds. ²³I will kill her children with death, and all the churches shall know that I am He who searches the minds and hearts. And I will give to each one of you according to your works.

²⁴"Now to you I say, and to the rest in Thyatira, as many as do not have this doctrine, who have not known the depths of Satan, as they say, I will put on you no other burden. ²⁵But hold fast what you have till I come. ²⁶And he who overcomes, and keeps My works until the end, to him I will give power over the nations—

²⁷'He shall rule them with a rod of iron;

They shall be dashed to pieces like the potter's vessels'—

as I also have received from My Father; ²⁸and I will give him the morning star.

²⁹He who has an ear, let him hear what the Spirit says to the churches.'"

EXPLORATION

1. For what was the church at Thyatira commended?

Love
Faith
Patience
Works

2. The church at Thyatira worked hard but let a false teacher slip in. Why did Jesus hold this against them?

They allowed it

3. What was the danger of Jezebel's false teaching and prophesying?

She will be thrown on a bed of suffering
Cast into a sickbed
Great tribulation
Her children will be killed with
Death

4. How could some members of the church be deceived by Jezebel's teaching?

Not Knowing Scripture

5. What facts do you learn about future judgment? How will we be judged?

INSPIRATION

How does God use Satan to do the work of heaven? God uses Satan to: *Revive the faithful*.

We all have the devil's disease. Even the meekest among us have a tendency to think too highly of ourselves. Apparently Paul did. His resume was impressive: a personal audience with Jesus, a participant in heavenly visions, an apostle chosen by God, an author of the Bible. He healed the sick, traveled the world, and penned some of history's greatest documents. Few could rival his achievements. And maybe he knew it. Perhaps there was a time when Paul began to pat himself on the back. God, who loved Paul and hates pride, protected Paul from the sin. And he used Satan to do it.

"To keep me from becoming conceited because of these surpassingly great revelations, there was given me a thorn in my flesh, a messenger from Satan to torment me" (2 Cor. 12:7 NIV).

We aren't told the nature of the thorn, but we are told its purpose—to keep Paul humble. We are also told its origin—a messenger from Satan. The messenger could have been a pain, a problem or a person who was a pain. We don't know. But we do know the messenger was under God's control. Please note verse eight, "Three times I pleaded with the Lord to take it away from me. But he said to me, 'My grace is sufficient for you, my power is made perfect in weakness.'" Satan and his forces were simply a tool in the hand of God to strengthen a servant. (From *The Great House of God* by Max Lucado)

REACTION

6. How did God use Satan's representative, Jezebel, to accomplish his purposes in Thyatira, much as he did with Paul's thorn in the flesh mentioned above?

7. Why did the church allow Jezebel to continue teaching?

8. What attitudes or activities are you condoning that are not pleasing to God?

9. How can you determine the sometimes subtle differences between Christian teaching and false doctrine?

10. Christ searches all our thoughts and intentions. How does knowing this help you avoid being deceived by false teaching?

11. How can you "hold fast" and remain loyal to Christ this week?

LIFE LESSONS

The charge against the church of Thyatira had to do with minimizing the effects of sexual immorality. In modern times, the world has not ceased to downplay the devastation caused by sexual immorality. When the followers of Jesus begin to shrug their shoulders and even condone this kind of behavior in the world and among themselves, the church has lost a significant capacity to speak to the world.

We must be vigilant about our responses to the world's pressure to "lighten up" when it comes to caring deeply about the way we conduct relationships.

DEVOTION

Jesus, help us to sharpen our listening skills to hear your true voice amid the voices of pressure, success, and power. Give us the strength to say no to the world and yes to you.

For more Bible passages on discernment, see Matthew 7:1–5; Ephesians 6:10–20; Philippians 1:9–11; Hebrews 5:12–14; James 1:5.

To complete the book of Revelation during this twelve-part study, read Revelation 2:18–29.

JOURNALING

Am I condoning some attitudes or activities that are not pleasing to God? How can I be more discerning?

PERSEVERANCE

MAX
LUCADO

REFLECTION

If at first you don't succeed, what do you do? The idea of perseverance appeals
to a high sense of personal integrity, but actually *persevering* takes real character.
Think of a commitment or project you wanted to quit but didn't. What was the
result of your perseverance?

SITUATION

Following messages to the churches in Ephesus, Smyrna, Pergamum, and
Thyatira, Jesus' words to the church in Sardis were chilling. This church had a
reputation that was only a sham. He called the church dead. He could commend
only a few believers who kept the faith. Then Jesus turned to the sixth church.
He issued a glowing report on the believers in Philadelphia.

OBSERVATION

Read Revelation 3:7–13 from the NCV or NKJV.

NCV

⁷"Write this to the angel of the church in Philadelphia:

"This is what the One who is holy and true, who holds the key of David, says. When he opens a door, no one can close it. And when he closes it, no one can open it. ⁸I know what you do. I have put an open door before you, which no one can close. I know you have a little strength, but you have obeyed my teaching and were not afraid to speak my name. ⁹Those in the synagogue that belongs to Satan say they are Jews, but they are not true Jews; they are liars. I will make them come before you and bow at your feet, and they will know that I have loved you. ¹⁰You have obeyed my teaching about not giving up your faith. So I will keep you from the time of trouble that will come to the whole world to test those who live on earth.

¹¹"I am coming soon. Continue strong in your faith so no one will take away your crown. ¹²I will make those who win the victory pillars in the temple of my God, and they will never have to leave it. I will write on them the name of my God and the name of the city of my God, the new Jerusalem, that comes down out of heaven from my God. I will also write on them my new name. ¹³Everyone who has ears should listen to what the Spirit says to the churches."

NKJV

⁷"And to the angel of the church in Philadelphia write,

'These things says He who is holy, He who is true, "He who has the key of David, He who opens and no one shuts, and shuts and no one opens": ⁸I know your works. See, I have set before you an open door, and no one can shut it; for you have a little strength, have kept My word, and have not denied My name. ⁹Indeed I will make those of the synagogue of Satan, who say they are Jews and are not, but lie—indeed I will make them come and worship before your feet, and to know that I have loved you. ¹⁰Because you have kept My command to persevere, I also will keep you from the hour of trial which shall come upon the whole world, to test those who dwell on the earth. ¹¹Behold, I am coming quickly! Hold fast what you have, that no one may take your crown. ¹²He who overcomes, I will make him a pillar in the temple of My God, and he shall go out no more. And I will write on him the name of My God and the name of the city of My God, the New Jerusalem, which comes down out of heaven from My God. And I will write on him My new name.

¹³"He who has an ear, let him hear what the Spirit says to the churches."'"

EXPLORATION

1. The church of Philadelphia was faithful to Christ's teachings. In what specific ways was this acknowledged?

> Obeyed teaching
> Not afraid to "speak my name"
> Did not give up faith

2. How is Jesus described here?

> Holy   Faithful
> True
> The One who holds the key of David
>   – Christs authority to open the
>   door of invitation to the
>   future kingdom; salvation

3. In what ways was Christ protecting the church of Philadelphia?

> Promised to protect them
> from the "hour of trial"

4. Christ promised rewards (a crown) to this church for holding fast. What other promises did he make (v. 12)?

He who overcomes,
I will make a pillar in the temple of
my God
I will write on him my new Name
of my God and the City of my God

5. Why did Christ value faithfulness in these early believers, and in us?

INSPIRATION

The economy of heaven, however, is refreshingly different. Heavenly rewards are not limited to a chosen few, but *"to all those who have waited with love for him to come again"* (2 Tim. 4:8 NCV). The three-letter word *all* is a gem. The winner's circle isn't reserved for a handful of the elite, but for a heaven full of God's children who *"will receive a crown of life that God has promised to those who love him"* (James 1:12 NIV).

From the mouth of Jesus, we hear a similar promise: The saved of Christ will receive their reward. *"When the master comes and finds the servant doing his work, the servant will be blessed"* (Matt. 24:46 NCV).

The promise is echoed in the epistles: *"The Lord will reward everyone for whatever good he does, whether he is slave or free"* (Eph. 6:8 NIV).

And in the beatitudes: *"Rejoice and be glad, because great is your reward in heaven"* (Matt. 5:12 NIV).

For all we don't know about the next life, this much is certain. The day Christ comes will be a day of reward. Those who went unknown on earth will be known in heaven. Those who never heard the cheers of men will hear the cheers of angels. Those who missed the blessing of a father will hear the blessing of their heavenly Father. The small will be great. The forgotten will be remembered. The unnoticed will be crowned and the faithful will be honored . . . You'll receive a crown—not just one crown but three. Would you like a preview?

The crown of life. *"Blessed is the man who perseveres under trial, because when he has stood the test, he will receive the crown of life that God has promised to those who love him"* (James 1:12 NIV).

To help you appreciate eternity, consider this rule of thumb: Heaven will be wonderful, not only because of what is present, but because of what is absent. Say that again? I'll be glad to. *Heaven will be wonderful, not only because of what is present, but because of what is absent.*

As the apostle John took notes on what he saw in heaven, he was careful to mention what was absent. Remember his famous list of "no mores"? God *"will wipe away every tear from their eyes, and there will be no more death, sadness, crying, or pain, because all the old ways are gone"* (Rev. 21:4 NCV).

Did you catch the first "no more"? There will be *no more death.* Can you imagine a world with no death, only life? If you can, you can imagine heaven. For citizens of heaven wear the crown of life. (From *When Christ Comes* by Max Lucado)

REACTION

6. Describe a time when you have struggled to remain faithful to God.

7. Who or what has helped you persevere in your faithfulness?

8. In what ways has God responded to your faithfulness?

I have confidence
I do not fear death
He is always there. He's the
one who is faithful

9. How has this passage encouraged you to persevere in faithfulness?

Hope that I will truly be rewarded in heaven and those who haven't been faithful will not receive the same reward?

10. Think of someone you know who is struggling to stay faithful to God. How can you encourage him or her?

By Example

11. In what ways has your church helped you stay faithful to God?

Pastors

Fellow Members

LIFE LESSONS

The challenge to stay true to Christ and practice faithfulness faces Christians every day. The church in Philadelphia reminds us of three crucial spiritual principles behind faithfulness: (1) acknowledging our own weakness and need; (2) obeying God's Word; and (3) claiming (not denying) Christ's name. We, too, can receive Christ's commendations and promises if we keep company with our brothers and sisters from Philadelphia.

DEVOTION

Father, we persevere in faithfulness because our hopes are set on heaven. We hold firmly to your promise of eternal life. Encourage us to stay focused on you when times grow difficult.

For more Bible passages on perseverance, see Matthew 24:12–13; Mark 13:12–13; Romans 5:3–4; 1 Thessalonians 1:2–7; 1 Timothy 6:11–12; James 1:2–4.

To complete the book of Revelation during this twelve-part study, read Revelation 3:1–13.

JOURNALING

What makes it difficult for me to persevere through trials?

VIBRANT
FAITH

MAX
LUCADO

REFLECTION

Like your physical body, the body of Christ has an ideal healthy temperature. Jesus knows what it is, and his Spirit sets the temperature. Higher than normal temperature indicates a battle with disease; lower than normal indicates a dangerous exposure to elements. When the body gets too cold, it dies. A lukewarm body is a body in trouble. If your church had a temperature, what would it be?

SITUATION

When it comes to Laodicea, the last church turned out to be the least. As the seventh church on the Lord's list, Laodicea stood distinctly apart from the others. This church received no positive feedback. The church had not stepped forward; it had not stepped backward. It was immobilized—lukewarm. Jesus' response to them was devastating.

OBSERVATION

Read Revelation 3:14–22 from the NCV or the NKJV.

NCV

14"Write this to the angel of the church in Laodicea:

"The Amen, the faithful and true witness, the beginning of all God has made, says this: *15*I know what you do, that you are not hot or cold. I wish that you were hot or cold! *16*But because you are lukewarm—neither hot, nor cold—I am ready to spit you out of my mouth. *17*You say, 'I am rich, and I have become wealthy and do not need anything.' But you do not know that you are really miserable, pitiful, poor, blind, and naked. *18*I advise you to buy from me gold made pure in fire so you can be truly rich. Buy from me white clothes so you can be clothed and so you can cover your shameful nakedness. Buy from me medicine to put on your eyes so you can truly see.

19"I correct and punish those whom I love. So be eager to do right, and change your hearts and lives. *20*Here I am! I stand at the door and knock. If you hear my voice and open the door, I will come in and eat with you, and you will eat with me.

21"Those who win the victory will sit with me on my throne in the same way that I won the victory and sat down with my Father on his throne. *22*Everyone who has ears should listen to what the Spirit says to the churches."

NKJV

14"And to the angel of the church of the Laodiceans write,

'These things says the Amen, the Faithful and True Witness, the Beginning of the creation of God: *15*I know your works, that you are neither cold nor hot. I could wish you were cold or hot. *16*So then, because you are lukewarm, and neither cold nor hot, I will vomit you out of My mouth. *17*Because you say, 'I am rich, have become wealthy, and have need of nothing'—and do not know that you are wretched, miserable, poor, blind, and naked—*18*I counsel you to buy from Me gold refined in the fire, that you may be rich; and white garments, that you may be clothed, that the shame of your nakedness may not be revealed; and anoint your eyes with eye salve, that you may see. *19*As many as I love, I rebuke and chasten. Therefore be zealous and repent. *20*Behold, I stand at the door and knock. If anyone hears My voice and opens the door, I will come in to him and dine with him, and he with Me. *21*To him who overcomes I will grant to sit with Me on My throne, as I also overcame and sat down with My Father on His throne."

22"He who has an ear, let him hear what the Spirit says to the churches.'"

EXPLORATION

1. Christ accused the church of Laodicea of becoming lukewarm. Why would God want our faith to be hot or cold, rather than lukewarm?

2. What do you learn here about who Jesus is and what he does?

3. Why did Christ call this church wretched, miserable, poor, blind, and naked if they were wealthy?

4. What was Jesus' counsel to these believers? What would it take for this church to get out of their miserable state?

5. What factors might have enabled this church to become lukewarm in their faith?

INSPIRATION

Consider the Laodicean church. This church was wealthy and self-sufficient. But the church had a problem—hollow, fruitless faith. "I know what you do," God spoke to this group, "that you are not hot nor cold. I wish that you were hot or cold! But because you are lukewarm—neither hot, nor cold—I am ready to spit you out of my mouth."

The literal translation is "to vomit." Why does the body vomit something? Why does it recoil violently at the presence of certain substances? Because they are incompatible with the body. Vomiting is the body's way of rejecting anything it cannot handle.

What's the point? God can't stomach lukewarm faith. He is angered by a religion that puts on a show but ignores the service. (From *And the Angels Were Silent* by Max Lucado)

REACTION

6. What characteristics might describe a lukewarm church today?

7. Why is it easier to rely on ourselves and our possessions than on God?

8. In what way is your current level of wealth affecting your spiritual devotion?

9. What areas in your relationship with God are easy to neglect? How can you keep your faith walk vibrant?

10. In what ways does this letter to the church of Laodicea speak to your church?

11. List some ways you can help your church reignite its zeal for God.

LIFE LESSONS

The age of tolerance and materialism in which we live might also be called the lukewarm age. People are not expected to believe anything firmly. It is so much safer to fill our lives with things and to remain neutral, inoffensive, and . . . lukewarm. This cultural spirit can easily slip into our faith walk. On a scale of 1 to 10, we may think our faith is a "safe 5." But now we know what Christ thinks of moderate faith. It comes as a shock to read this passage and find that he would prefer outright rejection to so-so commitment.

DEVOTION

Father, forgive us for relying on ourselves and temporary possessions. Help us to make our decisions based upon what is important and eternal. Thank you for loving us and calling us back to you.

For more Bible passages on hypocrisy, see Matthew 6:5; 7:1–5; Luke 12:1–3; James 4:8; 1 Peter 2:1.

To complete the book of Revelation during this twelve-part study, read Revelation 3:14–4:11.

JOURNALING

How can I reignite my zeal for God?

LESSON SEVEN

WORSHIPING GOD

MAX
LUCADO

REFLECTION

Worship can be as varied as the worshipers. But all worship revolves around the same purpose: giving God glory and praise! Think of a memorable worship experience. Was it something you prepared for, or an experience that caught you off guard? List the components that you can remember: participants, setting, and activities. Why was it so special?

SITUATION

Following the letters to the churches, John passed through a door into heaven (4:1). He was caught up in the Spirit and saw a throne, a glorious One on the throne, and twenty-four elders bowing and worshiping. The spotlight turned onto the great One on the throne and the ominous scroll he held. The news came that only One is worthy to open the scroll—the Lamb of God.

OBSERVATION

Read Revelation 5:8–14 from the NCV or the NKJV.

NCV

⁸*When he took the scroll, the four living creatures and the twenty-four elders bowed down before the Lamb. Each one of them had a harp and golden bowls full of incense, which are the prayers of God's holy people.* ⁹*And they all sang a new song to the Lamb:*

"You are worthy to take the scroll

and to open its seals,

because you were killed,

and with the blood of your death you bought people for God

from every tribe, language, people, and nation.

¹⁰*You made them to be a kingdom of priests for our God,*

and they will rule on the earth."

¹¹*Then I looked, and I heard the voices of many angels around the throne, and the four living creatures, and the elders. There were thousands and thousands of angels,* ¹²*saying in a loud voice:*

"The Lamb who was killed is worthy

to receive power, wealth, wisdom, and strength,

honor, glory, and praise!"

¹³*Then I heard all creatures in heaven and on earth and under the earth and in the sea saying:*

"To the One who sits on the throne

and to the Lamb

be praise and honor and glory and power

forever and ever."

¹⁴*The four living creatures said, "Amen," and the elders bowed down and worshiped.*

NKJV

⁸Now when He had taken the scroll, the four living creatures and the twenty-four elders fell down before the Lamb, each having a harp, and golden bowls full of incense, which are the prayers of the saints. ⁹And they sang a new song, saying:

"You are worthy to take the scroll,

And to open its seals;

For You were slain,

And have redeemed us to God by Your blood

Out of every tribe and tongue and people and nation,

¹⁰And have made us kings and priests to our God;

And we shall reign on the earth."

¹¹Then I looked, and I heard the voice of many angels around the throne, the living creatures, and the elders; and the number of them was ten thousand times ten thousand, and thousands of thousands, ¹²saying with a loud voice:

"Worthy is the Lamb who was slain

To receive power and riches and wisdom,

And strength and honor and glory and blessing!"

¹³And every creature which is in heaven and on the earth and under the earth and such as are in the sea, and all that are in them, I heard saying:

"Blessing and honor and glory and power

Be to Him who sits on the throne,

And to the Lamb, forever and ever!"

¹⁴Then the four living creatures said, "Amen!" And the twenty-four elders fell down and worshiped Him who lives forever and ever.

EXPLORATION

1. Christ was the object of this worship experience. Why was Christ, the Lamb, being worshiped?

2. Music was a part of this worship experience. How does music help us worship?

3. What attributes of God do you concentrate on in your worship? How do you see them reflected in this passage?

4. How would you feel if you were sharing in this heavenly worship service?

5. What do you think it will be like to worship God forever?

INSPIRATION

When you recognize God as Creator, you will admire him. When you recognize his wisdom, you will learn from him. When you discover his strength, you will rely on him. But only when he saves you will you worship him.

It's a "before and after" scenario. Before your rescue, you could easily keep God at a distance. Comfortably dismissed. Neatly shelved. Sure he was important, but so was your career. Your status. Your salary. He was high on your priority list, but he shared the spot with others.

Then came the storm . . . the rage . . . the fight . . . the ripped moorings . . . the starless night. Despair fell like a fog; your bearings were gone. In your heart, you knew there was no exit.

Turn to your career for help? Only if you want to hide from the storm . . . not escape it. Lean on your status for strength? A storm isn't impressed with your title. Rely on your salary for rescue? Many try . . . many fail.

Suddenly you are left with one option: God.

And when you ask . . . genuinely ask . . . he will come.

And from that moment on, he is not just a deity to admire, a teacher to observe, or a master to obey. He is the Savior. The Savior to be worshiped. (From *In the Eye of the Storm* by Max Lucado)

REACTION

6. Why is worship important for believers in general? For you?

7. What can block your worship of Christ?

8. Because you realize that Christ was slain to redeem you, how will you live differently?

9. What are some different aspects of worship?

10. In what ways do you worship Christ in your church?

11. What style of worship do you enjoy the most?

LIFE LESSONS

Worship on this side of eternity is "rehearsal" for worship in eternity. We are practicing at giving attention to the One who is worthy, our wonderful Savior. This doesn't come easy to those who spend much of their time giving attention to things without eternal worth. The apostle John's vision reveals glimpses of heavenly worship that can inspire and guide our efforts to lavish praise and honor on our Creator, Redeemer, and Lord.

DEVOTION

God, we cannot thank you enough for the redemption of your blood. We lift up our voices in praise to you, for you are worthy to receive honor, glory, and blessing. Holy, holy, holy are you, the Lord God Almighty!

For more Bible passages on worship, see 1 Chronicles 13:8; Psalms 81:1–4; 100:1–5; Matthew 2:11; John 4:21–24.

To complete the book of Revelation during this twelve-part study, read Revelation 5:1–11:19.

JOURNALING

How can I incorporate more worship into my daily routine?

L E S S O N   E I G H T

SONGS OF
VICTORY

MAX
LUCADO

REFLECTION

Winning can be fun, satisfying, and thrilling. Whether we ourselves are on the winning team or have merely cheered for the winning team, we feel included in the victory. Think of the last time your favorite team experienced a major victory. How was the team honored? How did you participate in honoring them?

SITUATION

Several chapters of John's vision have passed, focusing on the seals, trumpets, and bowls of God's judgment that have been poured out on the earth. As stunned and disheartened as we may sometimes be over the violence people commit against other people, the time is coming for a settling of accounts. God will bring justice to the earth. Then there will be time for a great celebration. God will make all things new. After judgment, worship will resume.

OBSERVATION

Read Revelation 19:1–10 from the NCV or the NKJV.

NCV

¹After this vision and announcement I heard what sounded like a great many people in heaven saying:

> *"Hallelujah!*
>
> *Salvation, glory, and power belong to our God,*
>
> *²because his judgments are true and right.*
>
> *He has punished the prostitute*
>
> *who made the earth evil with her sexual sin.*
>
> *He has paid her back for the death of his servants."*

³Again they said:

"Hallelujah!

She is burning, and her smoke will rise forever and ever."

⁴Then the twenty-four elders and the four living creatures bowed down and worshiped God, who sits on the throne. They said:

"Amen, Hallelujah!"

⁵Then a voice came from the throne, saying:

"Praise our God, all you who serve him

and all you who honor him, both small and great!"

⁶Then I heard what sounded like a great many people, like the noise of flooding water, and like the noise of loud thunder. The people were saying:

"Hallelujah!

Our Lord God, the Almighty, rules.

⁷Let us rejoice and be happy

and give God glory,

because the wedding of the Lamb has come,

and the Lamb's bride has made herself ready.

⁸Fine linen, bright and clean, was given to her to wear."

(The fine linen means the good things done by God's holy people.)

⁹And the angel said to me, "Write this: Happy are those who have been invited to the wedding meal of the Lamb!" And the angel said, "These are the true words of God."

¹⁰Then I bowed down at the angel's feet to worship him, but he said to me, "Do not worship me! I am a servant like you and your brothers and sisters who have the message of Jesus. Worship God, because the message about Jesus is the spirit that gives all prophecy."

NKJV

¹After these things I heard a loud voice of a great multitude in heaven, saying, "Alleluia! Salvation and glory and honor and power belong to the Lord our God! ²For true and righteous are His judgments, because He has judged the great harlot who corrupted the earth with her fornication; and He has avenged on her the blood of His servants shed by her." ³Again they said, "Alleluia! Her smoke rises up forever and ever!" ⁴And the twenty-four elders and the four living creatures fell down and worshiped God who sat on the throne, saying, "Amen! Alleluia!" ⁵Then a voice came from the throne, saying, "Praise our God, all you His servants and those who fear Him, both small and great!"

⁶*And I heard, as it were, the voice of a great multitude, as the sound of many waters and as the sound of mighty thunderings, saying, "Alleluia! For the Lord God Omnipotent reigns! ⁷Let us be glad and rejoice and give Him glory, for the marriage of the Lamb has come, and His wife has made herself ready." ⁸And to her it was granted to be arrayed in fine linen, clean and bright, for the fine linen is the righteous acts of the saints.*

⁹*Then he said to me, "Write: 'Blessed are those who are called to the marriage supper of the Lamb!'" And he said to me, "These are the true sayings of God." ¹⁰And I fell at his feet to worship him. But he said to me, "See that you do not do that! I am your fellow servant, and of your brethren who have the testimony of Jesus. Worship God! For the testimony of Jesus is the spirit of prophecy."*

EXPLORATION

1. Why is everyone celebrating in this passage?

2. Christ was honored for his triumph. How do we honor his triumphs today?

3. What is special about being invited to the wedding feast?

4. When was the last time you were a part of a celebration of victory over sin?

5. Why is Christ's victory an eternal one?

INSPIRATION

Triumph is a precious thing. We honor the triumphant. The gallant soldier sitting astride his steed. The determined explorer returning from his discovery. The winning athlete holding aloft the triumphant trophy of victory. Yes, we love triumph.

Triumph brings with it a swell of purpose and meaning. When I'm triumphant, I'm worthy. When I'm triumphant, I count. When I'm triumphant, I'm significant.

Triumph is fleeting, though. Hardly does one taste victory before it is gone; achieved, yet now history. No one remains champion forever. Time for yet another conquest, another victory. Perhaps this is the absurdity of Paul's claim: *"But thanks be to God, who always leads us in triumphal procession"* (2 Cor. 2:14 NIV).

The triumph of Christ is not temporary. "Triumphant in Christ" is not an event or an occasion. It's not fleeting. To be triumphant in Christ is a life-style . . . a state of being! To triumph in Christ is not something we do; it's something we are.

Here is the big difference between victory in Christ and victory in the world: A victor in the world rejoices over something he *did*—swimming the English Channel, climbing Mt. Everest, making a million. But the believer rejoices over who he *is*—a child of God, a forgiven sinner, an heir of eternity. As the hymn goes, "heir of salvation, purchase of God, born of his Spirit, washed in his blood."

Nothing can separate us from our triumph in Christ. Nothing! Our triumph is not based upon our feelings, but upon God's gift. Our triumph is based not upon our perfection, but upon God's forgiveness. How precious is this triumph! For even though we are pressed on every side, the victory is still ours. Nothing can alter the loyalty of God . . . "Triumphant in Christ." It is not something we do. It's something we are. (From *Shaped by God* by Max Lucado)

REACTION

6. On what can we base our victory in life?

7. Over what can we claim victory in Christ?

8. How can we praise God for his victory?

9. In what ways are you placing too much emphasis upon your own victories? How could you "lose" and Christ still win?

10. In what ways can you share Christ's victory with others?

11. How does understanding Christ's victory help you persevere through times of defeat?

LIFE LESSONS

It's worth taking note of Christ's victories, because we are going to be singing about them in eternity. We have to consider not using the term "singing for a long time," because "time" will not mean anything in an eternal place. Our activities will be measured some other way. But the content of our heavenly worship songs we can imagine and practice. Think with gratitude about all that Christ has done for you, and then develop an ever-expanding list of victories that he has achieved on your behalf.

DEVOTION

We give you praise, Jesus. We honor and glorify your name. May our voices be lifted up as we thank you, worship you, and glorify your name forever.

For more Bible passages on victory, see Psalm 21:1–13; Hebrews 11:32–12:2; 1 John 3:8–9; Revelation 2:7.

To complete the book of Revelation during this twelve-part study, read Revelation 12:1–19:10.

JOURNALING

I praise God for his victory over evil because . . .

LESSON NINE

THE BEAST'S DEFEAT

MAX
LUCADO

REFLECTION

Given the struggles and setbacks we experience in life, it is sometimes difficult to remember that the victory has already been won. It was won by Christ at the cross. We can participate in the victory; but we can't alter the outcome. Have you ever competed in an event, knowing you would win? How did that affect your performance?

SITUATION

The victory has been won, but in John's vision a great battle was joined on the earth. The great Captain rode a white horse, and out of his mouth came a great sword that will assure the final outcome. John stood in awe and watched God's army crush the fierce armies of evil. All that is left is food for the birds.

OBSERVATION

Read Revelation 19:11–20 from the NCV or the NKJV.

NCV

11Then I saw heaven opened, and there before me was a white horse. The rider on the horse is called Faithful and True, and he is right when he judges and makes war. 12His eyes are like burning fire, and on his head are many crowns. He has a name written on him, which no one but himself knows. 13He is dressed in a robe dipped in blood, and his name is the Word of God. 14The armies of heaven, dressed in fine linen, white and clean, were following him on white horses. 15Out of the rider's mouth comes a sharp sword that he will use to defeat the nations, and he will rule them with a rod of iron. He will crush out the wine in the winepress of the terrible anger of God the Almighty. 16On his robe and on his upper leg was written this name: king of kings and lord of lords.

17Then I saw an angel standing in the sun, and he called with a loud voice to all the birds flying in the sky: "Come and gather together for the great feast of God 18so that you can eat the bodies of kings, generals, mighty people, horses and their riders, and the bodies of all people—free, slave, small, and great."

19Then I saw the beast and the kings of the earth. Their armies were gathered together to make war against the rider on the horse and his army. 20But the beast was captured and with him the false prophet who did the miracles for the beast. The false prophet had used these miracles to trick those who had the mark of the beast and worshiped his idol. The false prophet and the beast were thrown alive into the lake of fire that burns with sulfur.

NKJV

11Now I saw heaven opened, and behold, a white horse. And He who sat on him was called Faithful and True, and in righteousness He judges and makes war. 12His eyes were like a flame of fire, and on His head were many crowns. He had a name written that no one knew except Himself. 13He was clothed with a robe dipped in blood, and His name is called The Word of God. 14And the armies in heaven, clothed in fine linen, white and clean, followed Him on white horses. 15Now out of His mouth goes a sharp sword, that with it He should strike the nations. And He Himself will rule them with a rod of iron. He Himself treads the winepress of the fierceness and wrath of Almighty God. 16And He has on His robe and on His thigh a name written:

KING OF KINGS

AND LORD OF LORDS.

17Then I saw an angel standing in the sun; and he cried with a loud voice, saying to all the birds that fly in the midst of heaven, "Come and gather together for the supper of the great God, 18that you may eat the flesh of kings, the flesh of captains, the flesh of mighty men, the flesh of horses and of those who sit on them, and the flesh of all people, free and slave, both small and great."

19And I saw the beast, the kings of the earth, and their armies, gathered together to make war against Him who sat on the horse and against His army. 20Then the beast was captured, and with him the false prophet who worked signs in his presence, by which he deceived those who received the mark of the beast and those who worshiped his image. These two were cast alive into the lake of fire burning with brimstone.

EXPLORATION

1. Why do you think Christ was portrayed in this passage as a warrior dressed in a robe dipped in blood?

2. In what ways does this description of Jesus differ from your view of him? What, for instance, is the significance of the sword coming from his mouth?

3. Why did the beast's armies believe they could defeat Christ?

4. Why did the armies not fight even though they were ready for battle?

5. What does it mean for us that the beast is defeated?

INSPIRATION

Imagine the event. You are before the judgment seat of Christ. The book is opened and the reading begins—each sin, each deceit, each occasion of destruction and greed. But as soon as the infraction is read, grace is proclaimed.

The result? God's merciful verdict will echo through the universe. For the first time in history, we will understand the depth of his goodness. Itemized grace. Catalogued kindness. Registered forgiveness. We will stand in awe as one sin after another is proclaimed, and then pardoned. Jealousies revealed, then removed. Infidelities announced, then cleansed. Lies exposed, then erased.

The devil will shrink back in defeat. The angels will step forward in awe. And we saints will stand tall in God's grace. As we see how much he has forgiven us, we will see how much he loves us. And we will worship him. We will join in the song of the saints: *"You are worthy to take the scroll and to open its seals, because you were killed, and with the blood of your death you bought people for God from every tribe, language, people, and nation"* (Rev. 5:9 NCV).

What a triumph this will be for our Master!

Perhaps you're thinking, *It will be a triumph for him, but humiliation for me.* No, it won't. Scripture promises, *"The one who trusts in him will never be put to shame"* (1 Pet. 2:6 NIV). (From *When Christ Comes* by Max Lucado)

REACTION

6. Knowing in advance that Christ will be victorious and triumphant, what sort of attitude should we have toward life?

7. Because we're assured that evil will ultimately be punished, how should we live differently?

8. In what ways does this passage inspire you?

9. What evidence can people see in your life that you're part of Christ's victorious army?

10. What does it mean to you that Jesus is Lord of lords and King of kings?

11. In what way does this passage alter your view of the end times?

LIFE LESSONS

The importance of knowing that our side wins in the end becomes clear when we face defeats in skirmishes and ambushes. They help us remember that victory comes from Christ and what he accomplished on the cross, not our much smaller victories that Christ helps us achieve. But we can certainly rejoice over Christ's victory. The outcome has been decided. Satan, evil, and death have been defeated. The turning point in history was the Cross. Everything else is "working out the details!" And we get to enjoy the benefits of Christ's victory for eternity.

DEVOTION

Jesus, you are truly the King of kings and Lord of lords. We give you praise and glory, for you have defeated the evil one. All victory belongs to you.

For more Bible passages on the beast's defeat, see Daniel 7:11, 23–27.

To complete the book of Revelation during this twelve-part study, read Revelation 19:11–20:15.

JOURNALING

How can I be a better soldier for Christ?

LESSON TEN

ALL THINGS
MADE NEW

MAX
LUCADO

REFLECTION

Most of the major events in life include built-in anticipation. Waiting is part of births, growing up, graduations, weddings—very few important things come instantly! Think of a time when you anticipated an upcoming event. What was the waiting like? How did you handle it?

SITUATION

By the time we reach Revelation 21, the battle is over. Death, Satan, and hell itself have been consigned to the lake of fire. It's time for something completely new. God has prepared a special place. It's more than any of us could conceive, and all who are his will be welcomed there.

OBSERVATION

Read Revelation 21:1–8 from the NCV or the NKJV.

NCV

¹*Then I saw a new heaven and a new earth. The first heaven and the first earth had disappeared, and there was no sea anymore.* ²*And I saw the holy city, the new Jerusalem, coming down out of heaven from God. It was prepared like a bride dressed for her husband.* ³*And I heard a loud voice from the throne, saying, "Now God's presence is with people, and he will live with them, and they will be his people. God himself will be with them and will be their God.* ⁴*He will wipe away every tear from their eyes, and there will be no more death, sadness, crying, or pain, because all the old ways are gone."*

⁵*The One who was sitting on the throne said, "Look! I am making everything new!" Then he said, "Write this, because these words are true and can be trusted."*

⁶*The One on the throne said to me, "It is finished. I am the Alpha and the Omega, the Beginning and the End. I will give free water from the spring of the water of life to anyone who is thirsty.* ⁷*Those who win the victory will receive this, and I will be their God, and they will be my children.* ⁸*But cowards, those who refuse to believe, who do evil things, who kill, who sin sexually, who do evil magic, who worship idols, and who tell lies—all these will have a place in the lake of burning sulfur. This is the second death."*

NKJV

¹*Now I saw a new heaven and a new earth, for the first heaven and the first earth had passed away. Also there was no more sea.* ²*Then I, John, saw the holy city, New Jerusalem, coming down out of heaven from God, prepared as a bride adorned for her husband.* ³*And I heard a loud voice from heaven saying, "Behold, the tabernacle of God is with men, and He will dwell with them, and they shall be His people. God Himself will be with them and be their God.* ⁴*And God will wipe away every tear from their eyes; there shall be no more death, nor sorrow, nor crying. There shall be no more pain, for the former things have passed away."*

⁵*Then He who sat on the throne said, "Behold, I make all things new." And He said to me, "Write, for these words are true and faithful."*

⁶*And He said to me, "It is done! I am the Alpha and the Omega, the Beginning and the End. I will give of the fountain of the water of life freely to him who thirsts.* ⁷*He who overcomes shall inherit all things, and I will be his God and he shall be My son.* ⁸*But the cowardly, unbelieving, abominable, murderers, sexually immoral, sorcerers, idolaters, and all liars shall have their part in the lake which burns with fire and brimstone, which is the second death."*

EXPLORATION

1. What is significant about the new city being described as a bride?

2. Why will this new earth be wonderful (vv. 3–4, 7–8)?

3. How would you describe the future citizens of the new city?

4. In what ways will our relationship with God be different in the new city?

5. Why will some people not be a part of the new city?

INSPIRATION

The most hopeful words of that passage from Revelation are those of God's resolve: "I am making everything new."

It's hard to see things grow old. The town in which I grew up is growing old. I was there recently. Some of the buildings are boarded up. Some of the houses are torn down. Some of my teachers are retired; some are buried. The old movie house where I took my dates has "For Sale" on the marquee, long since outdated by the newer theaters that give you eight choices. The only visitors to the drive-in theater are tumbleweeds and rodents. Memories of first dates and senior proms are weather-worn by the endless rain of years. High school sweethearts are divorced. A cheerleader died of an aneurysm. Our fastest halfback is buried only a few plots from my own father.

I wish I could make it all new again. I wish I could blow the dust off the streets. I wish I could walk through the familiar neighborhood, and wave at the familiar faces, and pet the familiar dogs, and hit one more home run in the Little League park. I wish I could walk down Main Street and call out to the merchants that have retired and open the doors that have been boarded up. I wish I could make everything new . . . but I can't . . .

I can't. But God can. "He restores my soul," wrote the shepherd. He doesn't reform; he restores. He doesn't camouflage the old; he restores the new. The Master Builder will pull out the original plan and restore it. He will restore the vigor. He will restore the energy. He will restore the hope. He will restore the soul.

When you see how this world grows stooped and weary and then read of a home where everything is made new, tell me, doesn't that make you want to go home?

What would you give in exchange for a home like that? Would you really rather have a few possessions on earth than eternal possessions in heaven? Would you really choose a life of slavery to passion over a life of freedom? Would you honestly give up all of your heavenly mansions for a second-rate sleazy motel on earth?

"Great," Jesus said, "is your reward in heaven." He must have smiled when he said that line. His eyes must have danced, and his hand must have pointed skyward.

For he should know. It was his idea. It was his home. (From *The Applause of Heaven* by Max Lucado)

REACTION

6. Describe the physical and emotional aspects of the new heaven and new earth.

7. In what ways does this passage encourage you? What are you looking forward to seeing or experiencing?

8. List some words that describe what you think it will be like to spend eternity with God.

9. What causes you to take your eyes off your wonderful future with God?

10. Why do we sometimes still reject Christ despite knowing about the end of the world?

II. List some of our responsibilities until the new heaven and new earth come.

LIFE LESSONS

We have a difficult time thinking about heaven without unconsciously "smuggling" earthbound thinking into it. All the elements of this life that make us tired, confused, bored, stressed, and overwhelmed will be gone. Just because we can't easily imagine ourselves in a heavenly setting doesn't mean that God can't change us to fit it perfectly! We can trust that God will take care of the details in ways that will surprise and delight us. We can give our full attention to opportunities God places in our lives to pass on the good news to others, in the hope that they, too, will be citizens of God's eternal kingdom.

DEVOTION

Father, we look forward to that new city where we will dwell with you. We hold to the promise that there will be no more sorrow or pain, and all things will be new. Keep our eyes focused on these things, that we can remain faithful to you.

For more Bible passages on the new heaven and new earth, see Hebrews 12:22–24; 2 Peter 3:10–13; Revelation 3:12.

To complete the book of Revelation during this twelve-part study, read Revelation 21:1–8.

JOURNALING

How can I prepare now for the new heaven and new earth?

THE NEW
JERUSALEM

MAX
LUCADO

REFLECTION

List two cities you would enjoy living in, including one or two positive and negative features about each one. Now, try to imagine a city with no evil whatsoever. How would you describe it? What makes it different even from the desirable cities you mentioned?

SITUATION

The amazing vision of the new city, New Jerusalem, continued. John was taken to a place where he could observe and examine the city itself. Full of wonders, his description stretches our imaginations to the limits. But included among the sights are notes of great comfort to us who expect to live there.

OBSERVATION

Read Revelation 21:9–27 from the NCV or the NKJV.

NCV

⁹Then one of the seven angels who had the seven bowls full of the seven last troubles came to me, saying, "Come with me, and I will show you the bride, the wife of the Lamb." ¹⁰And the angel carried me away by the Spirit to a very large and high mountain. He showed me the holy city, Jerusalem, coming down out of heaven from God. ¹¹It was shining with the glory of God and was bright like a very expensive jewel, like a jasper, clear as crystal. ¹²The city had a great high wall with twelve gates with twelve angels at the gates, and on each gate was written the name of one of the twelve tribes of Israel. ¹³There were three gates on the east, three on the north, three on the south, and three on the west. ¹⁴The walls of the city were built on twelve foundation stones, and on the stones were written the names of the twelve apostles of the Lamb.

15The angel who talked with me had a measuring rod made of gold to measure the city, its gates, and its wall. 16The city was built in a square, and its length was equal to its width. The angel measured the city with the rod. The city was twelve thousand stadia long, twelve thousand stadia wide, and twelve thousand stadia high. 17The angel also measured the wall. It was one hundred forty-four cubits high, by human measurements, which the angel was using. 18The wall was made of jasper, and the city was made of pure gold, as pure as glass. 19The foundation stones of the city walls were decorated with every kind of jewel. The first foundation was jasper, the second was sapphire, the third was chalcedony, the fourth was emerald, 20the fifth was onyx, the sixth was carnelian, the seventh was chrysolite, the eighth was beryl, the ninth was topaz, the tenth was chrysoprase, the eleventh was jacinth, and the twelfth was amethyst. 21The twelve gates were twelve pearls, each gate having been made from a single pearl. And the street of the city was made of pure gold as clear as glass.

22I did not see a temple in the city, because the Lord God Almighty and the Lamb are the city's temple. 23The city does not need the sun or the moon to shine on it, because the glory of God is its light, and the Lamb is the city's lamp. 24By its light the people of the world will walk, and the kings of the earth will bring their glory into it. 25The city's gates will never be shut on any day, because there is no night there. 26The glory and the honor of the nations will be brought into it. 27Nothing unclean and no one who does shameful things or tells lies will ever go into it. Only those whose names are written in the Lamb's Book of Life will enter the city.

NKJV

9Then one of the seven angels who had the seven bowls filled with the seven last plagues came to me and talked with me, saying, "Come, I will show you the bride, the Lamb's wife." 10And he carried me away in the Spirit to a great and high mountain, and showed me the great city, the holy Jerusalem, descending out of heaven from God, 11having the glory of God. Her light was like a most precious stone, like a jasper stone, clear as crystal. 12Also she had a great and high wall with twelve gates, and twelve angels at the gates, and names written on them, which are the names of the twelve tribes of the children of Israel: 13three gates on the east, three gates on the north, three gates on the south, and three gates on the west.

14Now the wall of the city had twelve foundations, and on them were the names of the twelve apostles of the Lamb. 15And he who talked with me had a gold reed to measure the city, its gates, and its wall. 16The city is laid out as a square; its length is as great as its breadth. And he measured the city with the reed: twelve thousand furlongs. Its length, breadth, and height are equal. 17Then he measured its wall: one hundred and forty-four cubits, according to the measure of a man, that is, of an angel. 18The construction of its wall was of jasper; and the city was pure gold, like clear glass. 19The foundations of the wall of the city were adorned with all kinds of precious stones: the first foundation was jasper, the second sapphire, the third chalcedony, the fourth emerald, 20the fifth sardonyx, the sixth sardius, the seventh chrysolite, the eighth beryl, the ninth topaz, the tenth chrysoprase, the eleventh jacinth, and the twelfth amethyst.

21The twelve gates were twelve pearls: each individual gate was of one pearl. And the street of the city was pure gold, like transparent glass.

22But I saw no temple in it, for the Lord God Almighty and the Lamb are its temple. 23The city had no need of the sun or of the moon to shine in it, for the glory of God illuminated it. The Lamb is its light. 24And the nations of those who are saved shall walk in its light, and the kings of the earth bring their glory and honor into it. 25Its gates shall not be shut at all by day (there shall be no night there). 26And they shall bring the glory and the honor of the nations into it. 27But there shall by no means enter it anything that defiles, or causes an abomination or a lie, but only those who are written in the Lamb's book of Life.

EXPLORATION

1. Why would there be no need for a temple in this new city?

2. What parts of the spectacular description here are most meaningful to you?

3. What will be our role in the new city?

4. How can one's place in the city be secured?

5. What does this passage reveal about God's ultimate plan?

INSPIRATION

I'll be home soon. My plane is nearing San Antonio. I can feel the nose of the jet dipping downward. I can see the flight attendants getting ready. [My wife], Denalyn, is somewhere in the parking lot, parking the car and hustling the girls toward the terminal.

I'll be home soon. The plane will land. I'll walk down that ramp and hear my name and see their faces. I'll be home soon.

You'll be home soon, too. You may not have noticed it, but you are closer to home than ever before. Each moment is a step taken. Each breath is a page turned. Each day is a mile marked, a mountain climbed. You are closer to home than you've ever been.

Before you know it, your appointed arrival time will come; you'll descend the ramp and enter the City. You'll see faces that are waiting for you. You'll hear your name spoken by those who love you. And, maybe, just maybe—in the back, behind the crowds—the One who would rather die than live without you will remove his pierced hands from his heavenly robe and . . . applaud. (From *The Applause of Heaven* by Max Lucado)

REACTION

6. Why has God prepared the new city for us?

7. In what ways are you anticipating your new home?

8. What are you doing to prepare for your future in the new city?

9. Knowing that your future dwelling is this heavenly city, how has your perspective of your earthly home changed?

10. In what ways does the image of this future home help you deal with death?

11. How can this passage help you encourage someone who has lost important earthly possessions?

LIFE LESSONS

When we really see for ourselves the things that John saw, our "life lessons" will be over, replaced with the glories of our eternal home. The word *home* includes both the idea of place and of relationship. This is especially true of the New Jerusalem. It is a place we will live in relationship with God. Yet there's no temple. No "place" is needed to meet God—because God's glory is everywhere! We are growing in our desire for our eternal home when we are less concerned with what we will do there than with *who* is there. What joy there will be in the Lord's presence and in the grand company of others when that moment comes.

DEVOTION

God of heaven, we see your hand stretching as far as the east is from the west. Put your arms around us and embrace us, Father. Take us home. May we be yours forever.

For more Bible passages on the New Jerusalem, see Hebrews 12:22—24; Revelation 3:12.

To complete the book of Revelation during this twelve-part study, read Revelation 21:9—22:11.

JOURNALING

What difference should it make to my daily worries that I have a home secured in the new heaven and new earth?

JESUS IS
RETURNING

MAX
LUCADO

REFLECTION

It's probably anyone's guess which experience is harder—waiting to arrive at a destination or waiting for someone special to arrive. Think of a time when you were waiting for someone to return from a long journey. Describe your feelings. How did you spend your time waiting?

SITUATION

This amazing document provided to us through the last of the apostles has been called the Revelation of Jesus Christ, primarily because that's the opening phrase of the book. Since the word *of* in the title means "from" more than "about," we can think of the contents, particularly the last words, as a collection of "things Jesus revealed that he wants us to know." If this book was named for its main theme, we might call it the Return of Jesus Christ.

OBSERVATION

Read Revelation 22:12–17 from the NCV or the NKJV.

NCV

¹²"Listen! I am coming soon! I will bring my reward with me, and I will repay each one of you for what you have done. ¹³I am the Alpha and the Omega, the First and the Last, the Beginning and the End.

¹⁴"Happy are those who wash their robes so that they will receive the right to eat the fruit from the tree of life and may go through the gates into the city. ¹⁵Outside the city are the evil people, those who do evil magic, who sin sexually, who murder, who worship idols, and who love lies and tell lies.

¹⁶"I, Jesus, have sent my angel to tell you these things for the churches. I am the descendant from the family of David, and I am the bright morning star."

¹⁷The Spirit and the bride say, "Come!" Let the one who hears this say, "Come!" Let whoever is thirsty come; whoever wishes may have the water of life as a free gift.

NKJV

¹²"And behold, I am coming quickly, and My reward is with Me, to give to every one according to his work. ¹³"I am the Alpha and the Omega, the Beginning and the End, the First and the Last."

¹⁴Blessed are those who do His commandments, that they may have the right to the tree of life, and may enter through the gates into the city. ¹⁵But outside are dogs and sorcerers and sexually immoral and murderers and idolaters, and whoever loves and practices a lie.

¹⁶"I, Jesus, have sent My angel to testify to you these things in the churches. I am the Root and the Offspring of David, the Bright and Morning Star."

¹⁷And the Spirit and the bride say, "Come!" And let him who hears say, "Come!" And let him who thirsts come. Whoever desires, let him take the water of life freely.

EXPLORATION

1. Why is Jesus coming back?

2. Note all the names of Jesus. What do these names for Jesus, such as Alpha and Omega, Morning Star, etc., reveal about him?

3. What rewards will come to those who obey his commandments?

4. Why will evil people be left out of the city?

5. What are the benefits of eating from the tree of life and drinking the water of life?

INSPIRATION

In fact, it seems [God's] favorite word is *come.*

"*Come,* let us talk about these things. Though your sins are like scarlet, they can be as white as snow."

"All you who are thirsty, *come* and drink."

"*Come* to me, all of you who are tired and have heavy loads, and I will give you rest."

"*Come* to the wedding feast."

"*Come* follow me, and I will make you fish for people."

"Let anyone who is thirsty *come* to me and drink."

God is a God who invites. God is a God who calls. God is a God who opens the door and waves his hand pointing pilgrims to a full table.

His invitation is not just for a meal, however; it is for life. An invitation to come into his kingdom and take up residence in a tearless, graveless, painless world. Who can come? Whoever wishes. The invitation is at once universal and personal. (From *And the Angels Were Silent* by Max Lucado)

REACTION

6. In what ways does your life demonstrate that you believe Jesus is returning? How have others confirmed this?

7. What do you need to change to be prepared for Christ's return?

8. What reward would you like when Jesus returns?

9. Even though Jesus states that he is coming quickly, why has he delayed his return for nearly two thousand years?

10. What does this passage portray about God's salvation?

11. What is the contrast between the Root and Offspring of David and the Bright and Morning Star?

LIFE LESSONS

Jesus is coming back. The best way to wait is to keep busy, maintain wakefulness, and join the prayers of others who say, "Come, Lord Jesus." What kind of busyness? Knowing Jesus' commands and living them out each and every day. The assurance of meeting him should fuel our anticipation, as comforting and thrilling as coming home from a long journey—and more!

DEVOTION

Father, we are anticipating your return with much excitement. Help us to remain faithful to you while we wait. Come quickly, for we look forward to spending eternity with you.

For more Bible passages on Christ's return, see Daniel 7:13–14; Zechariah 2:10–11; 1 Thessalonians 4:13–5:1; 1 Peter 1:6–7.

To complete the book of Revelation during this twelve-part study, read Revelation 22:12–21.

JOURNALING

How can I daily remain faithful to Christ until he returns?

Lucado Life Lesson Series

The Gospel of Mark
1-4185-0942-6

The Gospel of Luke
1-4185-0943-4

The Gospel of John
1-4185-0944-2

Acts
1-4185-0945-0

Romans
1-4185-0946-9

1 Corinthians
1-4185-0947-7

Ephesians
1-4185-0953-1

Hebrews
1-4185-0955-8

James
1-4185-0956-6

1 & 2 Timothy and Titus
1-4185-0954-X

1 & 2 Peter
1-4185-0957-4

Revelation
1-4185-0958-2

*Revised and updated, the Lucado Life Lessons series is perfect
for small group or individual use and includes intriguing questions
that will take you deeper into God's Word.*

Thomas Nelson
Since 1798

Available at your local Christian Bookstore